THE TRUTH ABOUT
AMPHETAMINES
AND
STIMULANTS

NICOLETTE P. CONTI and PAULA JOHANSON

ROSEN
PUBLISHING®

New York

Published in 2012 by The Rosen Publishing Group, Inc.
29 East 21st Street, New York, NY 10010

First Edition

Library of Congress Cataloging-in-Publication Data

Conti, Nicolette P.
The truth about amphetamines and stimulants/Nicolette P. Conti, Paula
Johanson.—1st ed.
    p. cm.—(Drugs & consequences)
Includes bibliographical references and index.
ISBN 978-1-4488-5483-7 (library binding) 1. Amphetamines—Juvenile
literature. 2. Stimulants—Juvenile literature. 3. Amphetamine abuse—
Juvenile literature. I. Johanson, Paula. II. Title.
HV5822.A5C66 2012
613.8'4—dc22

2011000301

Manufactured in the United States of America

CPSIA Compliance Information: Batch #S11YA: For further information, contact Rosen Publishing, New York, New York, at 1-800-237-9932.

CONTENTS

A stimulant is something that eliminates fatigue. It can excite or arouse you to a higher level of activity. After a long, tough day at school or work, people may drink a sugary soft drink or a cup of coffee or eat a candy bar. They do this because they believe that these substances give them a boost of energy. The sugar in soda or candy or added to coffee gives them a lift that is easily used by their bodies. These foods might also contain a stimulant called caffeine. Caffeine keeps you alert and focused. In larger amounts, it can make you nervous and jittery.

Stimulants (also called uppers) are drugs that speed up the mind and body. Amphetamines are one kind of stimulant. They increase activity in the nervous system and cause a number of physical and psychological changes. Their effects resemble those of one of the body's natural hormones, adrenaline. But unlike natural hormones, stimulants can quickly cause serious harm to your body. Amphetamines are controlled substances in the United States, which means that they are a drug or chemical substance whose possession and use fall within the jurisdiction of federal and state laws. Although amphetamines are often prescribed by

Amphetamines, or "speed," are stimulants that target the central nervous system. They can be injected or snorted in powder form.

doctors to treat a wide range of conditions, including obesity, depression, and sleeping disorders, they are sometimes abused because of the rush they bring on. When amphetamines are abused, they can be extremely dangerous. They can cause hallucinations, headaches, and blurred vision, among other things. When these drugs wear off, users can feel exhausted, depressed, and anxious. Sometimes amphetamines can even cause death.

As a teenager, you may have been offered amphetamines to help you lose weight or stay awake during a study marathon for your exams. You may have used them. Or maybe you're just curious about them. Information about amphetamines and other stimulants can help you learn more about them and their effects on your body and behavior.

CHAPTER 1

A BRIEF HISTORY OF AMPHETAMINES AND STIMULANTS

Amphetamines were first synthesized in 1887, but weren't used medically until the 1930s, when doctors prescribed them to treat nasal congestion. Eventually, they were used to treat other conditions, including obesity, depression, and hyperactivity. It wasn't long before people discovered that the side effects—among them, excitement and alertness—could be pleasurable. That's when amphetamines began to be abused.

During the early decades of the twentieth century, the media labeled amphetamines a cure-all. Advertisements claimed that amphetamines would solve problems ranging from alcoholism to obesity. In the late 1950s, amphetamines were restricted; they could only be prescribed by doctors. Soon enough, people discovered that amphetamines could be found in some over-the-counter decongestant inhalers. Some began forming addictions to medications used to treat common cold symptoms.

Some students started abusing amphetamines because the drugs helped them stay awake to study. It wasn't long before young people learned that large doses produced a tremendous high. Amphetamines then became a popular recreational drug, nicknamed "speed."

A Growth in Popularity

By the early 1960s, amphetamine abuse was a major problem among young people. Hospitals and doctors began reporting many serious problems. Young people were suffering from heart attacks and strokes. Doctors and pharmacists noticed that young people were forging prescriptions for stimulants. Tighter limits were placed on the amounts of stimulants prescribed. The police began to crack down on drugstores that sold the drugs illegally.

In the 1970s, methamphetamines were considered drugs with little medical use, but a high potential for abuse. Illegal

A NEW BREED OF DRUGS

Mixing stimulants with heroin creates a powerful combination called a speedball. Crystal meth became popular in the 1960s as well. When chemists first created this mix, it was not a very pure drug, but it gave users the most intense high they had ever experienced.

By the early 1970s, so many people were addicted to stimulants that the U.S. government strictly limited the amounts that doctors could prescribe. As a result, speed labs spread across the country. Soon they were in almost every state. The Controlled Substances Act and the Comprehensive Drug Abuse Prevention and Control Act became law in 1970 to fight the abuse of drugs and other substances. The acts combined numerous laws to regulate the manufacture and distribution of narcotics, stimulants, depressants, hallucinogens, anabolic steroids, and chemicals used in the illegal production of controlled substances.

speed labs sprang up on the West Coast with many serious consequences. Although prescription stimulants were controlled by federal law, there were no such controls for the illegal labs. Many of them were dirty and did not use trained chemists. Soon hundreds of young people were arriving at hospitals sick or dying from drugs that had been made in speed labs.

Drug Labs

The creation of methamphetamine is usually done in small, illegal labs called meth labs. These labs exist in all areas of the

Drug labs, such as this meth lab, can be as, if not more, dangerous than the drugs they produce. The chemicals used are toxic and explosive if not mixed properly.

United States and in many other countries. Meth labs are easy to construct from commonly available materials.

A basic, small-scale meth lab requires the investment of only a few hundred dollars and can lead to enormous profits. These profits come with a high risk to the operators of the lab, their neighbors, and the clients or drug users. The chemicals commonly used in small speed labs include red phosphorus, hydrochloric acid, drain cleaner or lye, battery acid, lantern fuel, and antifreeze. Many of these substances are flammable, toxic, or caustic. Handling them can be very dangerous. When mixed together, they can also be explosive. Trained chemists take special precautions to protect themselves when they work with these chemicals. The operators of illegal speed labs seldom take the needed precautions.

Mishandling these kinds of chemicals results in explosions that can destroy buildings and kill operators and anyone else nearby. Because many meth labs are hidden in places such as old hotels, residential neighborhoods, and crowded trailer parks, there are usually large numbers of innocent people nearby.

Some of these chemicals produce toxic or poisonous fumes that can overcome and kill operators or escape and harm or kill someone nearby. Caustic chemicals used in the process of making speed can cause burns. If the caustic materials are dumped illegally, anyone can be affected. When law enforcement officers bust speed labs, they usually wear hazardous material suits to protect themselves from these dangerous chemicals.

Meth labs also have a negative impact on the environment. Because so many hazardous chemicals are used in the production of speed and so much hazardous waste is produced, there is a problem with the storage and disposal of these materials. In legitimate industries, hazardous chemicals and waste are properly stored or disposed of by incineration so that they do not pose a threat to people or the environment. Because meth labs are illegal, they do not follow these precautions.

Hazardous waste dumped in the trash can endanger anyone, including the people who collect the garbage. If the waste is poured down the drain, it can cause explosions in the sewage system. If the waste is dumped in storm sewers or on the ground, it can damage plant life and pollute nearby rivers and streams. This affects fish and animals in the river, as well as anyone who uses the water.

Hidden Dangers

Because speed is usually made in illegal labs, there is no quality control. This means that unlike prescription drugs sold in a pharmacy, there is no guarantee that an illegally made drug will be safe. Different chemicals used to make speed also contaminate it. Some contaminants are poison. Also, the drugs can be cut, or diluted, with additives ranging from flour to baby laxative or caffeine. Sometimes the capsules or tablets contain no amphetamines at all—only caffeine.

Most dealers buy from other dealers or from meth labs. Speed passes through many different hands before it reaches the user. A dealer sells drugs for money. He or she does not have the health and safety of the customer in mind. Dealers will lie, cheat, steal, and sometimes even kill to protect their business and continue selling drugs. Because dealers are not afraid of breaking the law, buyers have no way of knowing what they are buying. Because the drug business operates outside of the law, there are no money-back guarantees. There is also nothing

When buying drugs from dealers, you're gambling with your life. To make more profit, dealers often mix toxic fillers into the drugs they sell.

to protect you if you are wronged, cheated, or harmed during the illegal exchange. Anytime you buy drugs, you are taking a risk with your own health and safety.

One of the biggest dangers of amphetamines and related drugs is that new varieties are created all the time. Throughout the world, centers of the drug culture popularize different fad drugs. The use of some, such as crystal meth, has reached epidemic proportions.

You can help end the epidemic by choosing to keep drugs out of your life. Many people choose to stay drug-free after they learn how harmful drugs really are.

The Different Types of Amphetamines and Stimulants

Stimulants can occur naturally, as they do in caffeine, or they can be created in a laboratory. Amphetamines are synthetic—they're made in a laboratory. The term "amphetamine" is often used as a blanket name for several different stimulants.

Amphetamines are drugs used by doctors to treat hyperactivity in children, obesity, and sleeping disorders, as well as other conditions. They affect the heart, lungs, brain, and other organs. Amphetamines are usually taken in pill form.

Methamphetamine, also called methedrine, was developed from amphetamines and has a similar chemical makeup. But methamphetamine, a controlled substance (meaning that its possession and use is regulated under the Controlled Substances

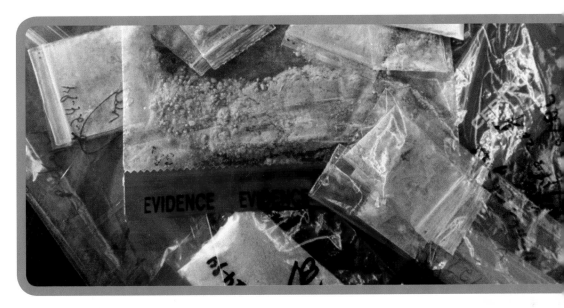

Methamphetamine often comes in clear plastic baggies in all different forms and colors. With no quality standards, users never truly know what they're getting.

Act passed by the U.S. Congress in 1970), is much stronger than amphetamines. Methamphetamine abusers are taking higher dosages than a doctor would prescribe.

Although methamphetamine has been used in the past for medicinal purposes in the form of crystalline hydrochloride (for example, as an appetite suppressant), today it is made mostly in illegal labs by manufacturers called cooks. Cooking methamphetamine is extremely dangerous: the chemical reaction caused by cooking methamphetamine creates acid fumes that are toxic. Some methamphetamine labs actually have exploded from the fumes coming into contact with a flame.

Crystal methamphetamine, also known as "ice," is one of the most dangerous forms of the drug because of its strength.

Ice is a pure, concentrated form of methamphetamine that looks like tiny bits of glass ("glass" is another name for it). The drug is smoked by being vaporized, then inhaled. There is a saying that ice is to methamphetamine as crack is to cocaine.

Crystal meth is a combination of methedrine and amphetamine. On the street or in treatment facilities, crystal meth and meth (methamphetamine) are one and the same drug. It is among the most abused of all the stimulants because it acts so quickly in the body. The high is almost instantaneous when crystal meth is injected into a vein or snorted. The high often is called a rush because it is so powerful.

Dealers often dilute cocaine or heroin with crystal meth because crystal meth is cheap. Often, people are given crystal meth but believe that they are using cocaine or heroin. This can lead to serious problems. If a person gets used to taking large doses of crystal meth and then takes a large dose of straight cocaine or heroin, he or she may overdose.

Because it reduces the appetite, phenmetrazine is prescribed by doctors to help people lose weight. It only comes in pill form. Abusers might swallow, crush and snort, or dissolve the pills and inject the solution into a vein.

The trade name for the drug methylphenidate is Ritalin. It is prescribed to treat attention deficit disorder (ADD) in children and narcolepsy (a sleeping disorder) in adults. When taken in large amounts, this drug acts very much like amphetamines. In some countries, methylphenidate can be bought over the counter. In the United States, it can be obtained only by prescription. The drug is available in pill form. It is usually swallowed, although some users dilute it and inject it into their veins. Ritalin is used in the treatment of ADD to help people remain alert and focus on complex tasks. It also helps calm young people who are hyperactive. Methylphenidate can be abused by people who do not have attention deficit disorder. It can have the opposite effect on these users, stimulating them and giving them a kind of euphoric high.

CHAPTER 2

THE EFFECTS ON THE BODY

Speed produces a feeling of euphoria and mental alertness. Taken orally, speed produces these effects within about fifteen to twenty minutes. If snorted, the effects begin in about three to five minutes. When speed is smoked or injected, the user experiences a rush almost immediately. Metabolism increases, as do blood pressure and heart rate. The user experiences a period of hyperactivity. He or she feels smart and assertive, as well as irritable and argumentative. As the effect wears off, the user crashes—that is, experiences a period of exhaustion and depression. At this point, the user feels a craving for the drug, wanting that high-energy feeling to overcome the depression. Speed users also tend to use more and more of the drug over time as they develop a tolerance for it. When the body becomes accustomed to a drug, larger and larger doses must be taken to achieve the same high. This pattern of reactions is typical for an abuser.

In the Short Term

When they are abused, stimulants have many negative effects on your mind and body. They change how you feel and how you act. When someone takes stimulants, he or she goes through immediate emotional and physical changes. The first feelings usually are of euphoria, alertness, and energy. But some users become angry, impatient, and even violent. Other effects include loss of appetite, inability to sleep, and mood swings.

Physical changes occur as well. Users have headaches, chest pain, or enlarged pupils. They also may talk very fast, make sudden movements, have a dry mouth, and clench or grind their teeth.

In addition, stimulants can kill instantly. Just one dose can cause heart failure, high fever, or a burst blood vessel in the brain. It is especially dangerous to use stimulants when exercising. Physical exertion causes one's blood pressure and heart rate to increase. The stimulants have already increased one's blood pressure and heart rate, so a stroke or heart attack can result from this overexertion.

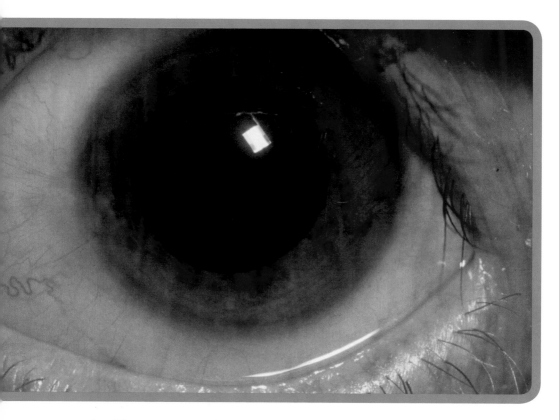

One of the many symptoms of stimulants is dilated pupils. This is often a tell-tale sign that police use to determine if a person is high on these drugs.

In the Long Term

The long-term effects of using stimulants are also devastating. They include weight loss, a rash that looks like chicken pox, boils, gum disease that may result in teeth falling out, distorted vision, lung problems, uncontrollable shaking, and brain damage.

There are many other dangers. Users may suffer from fever, convulsions, high blood pressure, depression, severe fatigue,

WHEN A FRIEND HAS AN ADDICTION

When I was about ten years old, I was like everyone else. I had my own little group of friends. We all would hang out together and have fun. But I never really had that one best friend, the one that you could hang out with forever, and never get sick of them. That all changed when I met Cameron. From the very beginning, we clicked like best friends do. We liked all the same games, had the same sense of humor, and we became inseparable. We were best friends for about a year, when things started to get really bad for him. His parents got divorced, eventually got back together, then divorced again. His mother got heavily involved in drugs and alcohol, and she fell into such a deep depression that it was rare for her to even get out of bed.

At this point, I knew that he was going to need his friends more than ever. His mom would tell him that he needed to just go find a place to stay. There would be lapses of weeks where he would stay at our house. We became family. I considered him my little brother because we had been through so much together. My parents weren't too support-ive of this; mostly they were mad at his mother for forcing them to pretty much take in another child to support. They let him stay because he literally had no other place to go. And they couldn't let him live on the streets.

We were best friends for five years. But slowly as we hit high school, we began to go our separate ways. The time between hanging out would grow from weeks, to months, to eventually the point where I didn't see him for a whole year. Then out of the blue he showed up, looking and acting completely different. I asked him how he was, and if he wanted to go find something to do. He said he couldn't because he was living with his dad now, and he was grounded. I, of course, asked him why. And he nonchalantly told me that his dad found drugs in his room.

I was shocked to learn this, but that was not even him hitting the bottom. A few weeks later, we found out that he had broken into our house and taken our computers and Xbox. He got away and left to some town that I had never even heard of before. The items were easily replaced, but all of this hit me like a bomb.

I couldn't figure out how my best friend, the person I looked at as my little brother, could do something like this to me. How could he completely turn on me like this? How could he hurt the family that picked him up when he was completely knocked down? I then started to feel guilty, as if he did this because I turned my back on him. I ditched him for the friends at my school, and I wasn't there to watch over him and make sure he stayed on a straight path. Was it my fault that he became a druggie and a thief?

I eventually came to the conclusion that it was not my fault. It was not my job to watch him and make sure that he would stay out of trouble all the time. I was not his mother. Although I still feel bad that things did not turn out differently, I know that I have to go my own way and live my own life, and make my own friends.

intense anger, nausea, vomiting, stomachaches, paranoia, blackouts, and suicidal tendencies.

Binging and Crashing

Some people may use speed only a few times. But speed is a powerful and seductive drug, and many people quickly graduate to a pattern of abuse that is described by the phrase "binge and crash." During a binge-and-crash cycle, the abuser usually takes speed repeatedly and continuously over a period of time that may vary from a weekend to as long as a couple of weeks.

TEN GREAT QUESTIONS TO ASK A DOCTOR

1. Does taking a prescription for amphetamines mean I'm going to become addicted?

2. Do you have any pamphlets or information you can give me to read later?

3. I'm really upset—is there someone who can talk with me about amphetamine use?

4. What can I do to stop taking amphetamines?

5. Where can I find a local twelve-step or self-help group?

6. Do you have to tell my parents about my drug use?

7. Can my friend/family member come with me to my self-help appointment?

8. Does it matter if I'm pregnant and taking amphetamines?

9. I have some other health concerns—could amphetamine use be affecting these?

10. What books about amphetamines and stimulants can I read to learn more?

The binge-and-crash user begins the cycle by taking speed for four to sixteen hours. As the high wears off and fatigue and depression set in, the user will try to maintain the high by repeatedly taking more speed. This is the binge phase of the cycle. The user may try to maintain a high for as long as three to fifteen days.

A user may accomplish this by tweaking, a process by which a user takes small doses of speed continuously to try to maintain an alert state and postpone the inevitable crash. This behavior may last for as long as two weeks. During this time, the user may get no real sleep at all. He or she is also likely to be irritable and paranoid during this time. He or she may behave violently, especially if other substances such as alcohol are being abused. The user may also experience hallucinations and paranoia, an intense and irrational fear of almost everyone and everything. Tweaking can also result in suicidal feelings. The tweaker craves more speed but cannot re-create the initial high because his or her body is already overloaded with stimulants. This often produces intense feelings of frustration. The frustration may lead to unpredictable, violent, and self-destructive actions.

Tweakers can appear normal at first glance—their eyes are clear, their speech is concise and coherent, and their movements are brisk—but if you look closer, you can tell that something isn't right. Usually the user's eyes will be moving much faster than normal. The user's voice might have a slight quiver, and his or her bodily movements might be quick and jerky. Because of their unpredictable and possibly violent

People who use amphetamines and stimulants often experience aggressive behavior, which can take the form of road rage.

behavior, tweakers can be dangerous. They are often found at raves, or all-night parties. Tweakers are also often involved in traffic accidents and are responsible for many of the incidents classified as road rage.

Tweakers may also take part in spur-of-the-moment crimes such as purse snatchings, muggings, or assaults. They do these desperate and illegal things for money to support their habit.

After the tweaking phase, the abuser finally crashes, mentally and physically exhausted. Usually, he or she will sleep heavily for long periods, fatigued and depressed. After a few days or perhaps a week, the abuser may be ready for another cycle of binging and crashing.

People who go through these long cycles of binging and crashing are called speed freaks. Because they consume such large amounts of speed, it is not uncommon for them to experience hallucinations. One common hallucination is the experience of crank bugs. The user feels as if bugs are crawling all over the body. He or she may violently scratch at the skin, which leads to open wounds and ugly scars. If you snort speed, your nasal passages can become burned and scarred. Other common signs of heavy speed use are extreme weight loss, pale skin, excessive sweating, body odor, and discolored teeth.

If you are able to break the binge-and-crash cycle, you will suffer from withdrawal symptoms. The symptoms of withdrawal are powerful depression and lethargy. Because the pleasure centers of the brain have been overstimulated and overworked by the drug, one symptom of withdrawal is the temporary inability to feel pleasure. These unpleasant feelings may cause the abuser to become suicidal. The desire to get rid of unpleasant feelings is so strong that you are almost certain to want to get high again. For this reason, overcoming an addiction to speed is usually a complicated psychological process. You must overcome your dependence on the drug for a sense of well-being.

CHAPTER 3

HOW AMPHETAMINES AND STIMULANTS AFFECT THE BRAIN

The brain is the organ of thought and consciousness. The central nervous system allows the brain to control and regulate all other functions of your body. All thoughts, memories, sensations, and decisions to act are processed by your brain. Your brain also controls all sorts of bodily functions that you don't have to think about, like breathing and swallowing and blinking your eyes. Through its control of the body's glands, the brain regulates the release of

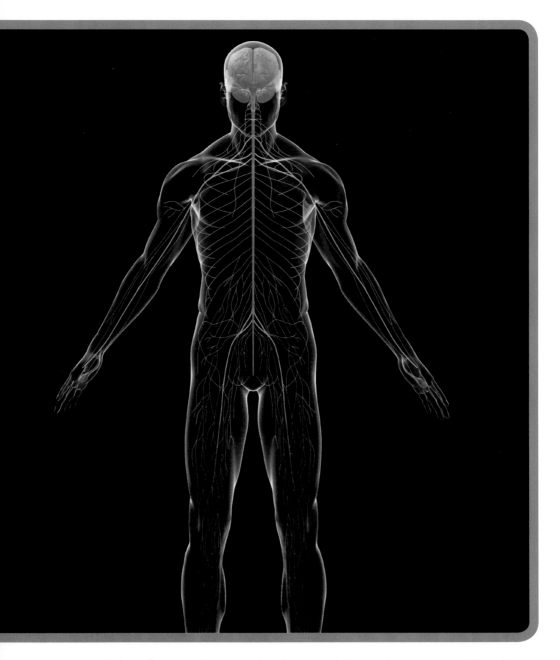

The brain communicates with the rest of the body through the central nervous system. Effects of amphetamines and stimulants can be transmitted throughout the body.

chemicals. These chemicals affect emotions, moods, and the body's metabolism. The brain controls everything and carries within itself everything that makes up your unique personality.

The brain doesn't have to stop working completely to cause you problems. When it is exposed to drugs or toxic chemicals, almost anything can happen. Your thoughts can lose touch with reality. They can become disconnected and irrational. Your memories can disappear. You can lose control of your emotions and moods. Everything around you can become distorted and seem inaccurate. Normal sensations such as sights, sounds, smells, and tastes can become terrifying.

How the Brain Communicates

The brain is made up of hundreds of billions of separate nerve cells, or neurons. These neurons carry all the brain's signals. Each neuron has around its cell body a series of branching threads called dendrites. Dendrites pick up signals from other nerve cells. The signals are then transmitted down a long extension of the cell body called an axon, which also ends in a series of branching threads that pass the signals on to the dendrites of other neurons. In this way, passing from nerve cell to nerve cell, messages move back and forth from the brain to all parts of the body.

The key to everything lies in the tiny spaces between these branching threads of the neurons. These gaps, called synapses, are less than a millionth of an inch wide. Because there are

The brain's neurotransmitters allow a person to experience pleasure. When these transmitters are overloaded by drug use, they can become damaged.

hundreds of billions of nerve cells in your brain, each with hundreds or thousands of dendrites, the total number of synaptic gaps within your brain actually exceeds the number of elementary particles in the known universe.

A signal is transmitted electrically in a nerve cell from one end to the other. Neurotransmitters carry the signal from the end of one nerve cell, across the gap, and to another nerve cell.

Molecules of these chemicals are released from the signaling neuron and travel across the synapse to stimulate the next neuron. The molecules are then reabsorbed by the neuron that released them. There are many chemical neurotransmitters that perform different functions—substances like acetylcholine, epinephrine and norepinephrine, dopamine, and serotonin. Actually, more often than not, these substances carefully inhibit, rather than stimulate, other nerve cells and prevent too many signals from moving from neuron to neuron. This is so your brain is not overwhelmed by too many signals. If many nerve cells were carrying many signals at once, you would suffer a prolonged epileptic seizure. This seizure is a signal overload. So the purpose of many neurotransmitters is to act as information traffic cops and keep order in the brain.

Drugs like amphetamines are also chemicals. These chemicals are absorbed into the brain tissue and affect the way messages are carried across the synapses between nerve cells. Drugs can block the release of neurotransmitters. Consequently, signals would not be carried between nerve cells. Drugs can also stimulate the release of neurotransmitters in greater amounts. As a result, signals would be sent when they weren't meant to be. Nerve cells can be fooled by such drugs into triggering signals when they are not supposed to. Your nerve cells are literally out of control, and the effects might include hallucinations and mood swings, irrational thinking, loss of control over movement, violent convulsions, or unconsciousness and death.

When Things Go Out of Control

The nerve cells that regulate your bodily functions respond to the neurotransmitters norepinephrine, epinephrine, dopamine, and serotonin. Each of these chemicals has a different molecular structure. Each chemical stimulates a different response from the nerve cells.

Norepinephrine and epinephrine stimulate nerve cells associated with the body's fight-or-flight response to stress. The fight-or-flight response is part of the body's natural defense system. It prepares the body to protect itself by stimulating an aggressive reaction to stand and fight or a fearful reaction to flee from danger. These neurotransmitters cause the brain to focus its attention on the outside environment. They stimulate alertness to danger. They suppress your appetite and increase your heart rate to move blood quickly through the body. They increase your blood glucose level for a quick boost of energy. They also dilate, or widen, your breathing tubes to increase the oxygen supply in your blood.

The cost of this increased mental and physical efficiency is that your body needs more energy. Because the body is not taking in food, it is converting fat into energy. This is why speed causes weight loss. Your body no longer craves food. Your hormone levels are raised, and your body temperature is raised. This condition allows the body to function much more efficiently or with faster action (hyperactivity). This increased

People who use stimulants enough often experience what's called a crash once their bodies stop getting the drugs.

efficiency has its downside. Heightened concentration and readiness for danger drain the body of energy.

When the brain naturally invokes this response, it usually lasts no more than a couple of hours. Under normal circumstances, the body can quickly recover from this energy drain. When the body is stimulated with speed, this heightened state of alertness can last for eighteen to twenty-four hours or even for days or weeks if you continue tweaking to keep yourself high. This causes the body to draw deeply on its energy reserves. As these energy reserves are exhausted, the user eventually crashes.

A crash requires sleep and food to help the body recover. Hyperactive reactions brought about by stimulant use can easily get out of control and produce dramatic and violent symptoms.

The neurotransmitter dopamine has a different function. It causes a sense of pleasure and euphoria. It also controls the release of some hormones and affects your fine muscle control. The neurotransmitter serotonin is involved in the regulation of sleep and psychological moods. It also influences your body's ability to regulate temperature and control appetite. Stimulant use raises body temperature, speeding up the chemical reactions that release the energy stored in the body's fat cells, so serotonin makes more energy available for the body. This increased body temperature is dangerous, especially for athletes because exercise increases body temperature even more.

Immediate Dangers of Stimulants

You cannot predict the kind of physical dangers you might face when your mind has been taken over by feelings of paranoia and panic. Speed freaks have been known to do some pretty weird things. There are many more immediate dangers, especially if you overdose on speed. Because speed increases your blood pressure and heart rate, it can cause a heart attack or stroke. In low doses, speed would probably cause this only if you had a preexisting heart problem or weakened arteries— but you or your doctor might not know about these health problems. High or large doses of amphetamines can cause a heart attack or stroke in any user. Remember that when speed is purchased on the street, its purity is not known. As a result, it is difficult to estimate the strength of the dose you are taking. This increases the likelihood of a high dose or even an overdose.

An overdose from speed can happen in two different ways. A single, large dose may cause an overdose, or you may take repeated doses by tweaking until toxic levels are reached. Either way, the result is the same. Few people survive an overdose without immediate medical attention. When speed reaches a toxic level in the blood, you may experience seizures, convulsions, or a fatal elevation of body temperature. A speed overdose usually leaves the victim with severe damage to the brain or heart.

MYTHS & FACTS

MYTH Ritalin is safe for little kids to take, so it's safe for me to get high.

FACT Hyperactive children have a different metabolism, which reacts differently to stimulants. Pills are carefully prescribed to meet their special health needs. Adults and most children react differently to stimulants.

MYTH I need amphetamines to be able to perform well at my activities.

FACT If you need more of a stimulant than a cup of coffee and a meal, you will not be able to perform well at any activity. Doctors would not recommend using amphetamines so that you could do sports or work or other activities.

MYTH These amphetamines are from a drugstore, so I know they're good.

FACT Even prescription drugs must be taken under a doctor's care, not to get high on. Discuss with your doctor when and how you should take any drug, how it makes you feel, and whether it is doing what you and the doctor expect.

Lasting Effects of Stimulants

There are many dangers besides death or strokes associated with the long-term use of stimulants. The use of these drugs can cause a mental illness similar to paranoid schizophrenia (people suffering from this disorder falsely believe they are being persecuted or they are a famous or important person). Malnutrition is common among users due to appetite suppression. Long-term use also weakens the immune system. The user will then develop diseases more easily. Injecting speed and sharing needles can lead to infections and blood-borne diseases such as AIDS and hepatitis. Blood vessels may become blocked, which may cause the loss of an arm or leg or increase the possibility of a heart attack later in life. Finally, because of heightened irritability and aggression, users may commit crimes or cause injuries to innocent people.

The use of stimulants during pregnancy can affect an unborn baby. Because the drugs travel through the bloodstream, they pass through the placenta to the fetus. Speed, for example, causes birth defects such as heart defects, cleft palates, and physical and mental disorders. It may cause the baby to be born addicted to speed. The baby will suffer withdrawal symptoms from the moment of birth.

CHAPTER 4

ADDICTION TO AMPHETAMINES AND STIMULANTS

Stimulants create a cycle of feelings and behavior in users. When someone is high on amphetamines, he or she feels invincible, happy, and alert. But after those feelings fade, the person crashes and feels depressed, anxious, and nervous. In order to feel good again, he or she will take more stimulants and then crash again. That's the cycle: get high, crash, get high, crash. This cycle of getting high and crashing puts a person on the road to addiction. Once a person starts using stimulants, his or her body will need more and more. Soon, the craving for stimulants will take control of the person's life.

Addiction can be both physical and psychological. A user can psychologically depend on the high brought on by stimulants. A person can become physically addicted because he or she develops a tolerance to the drug, needing larger and larger doses in order to get the same high.

People sometimes use stimulants over and over without stopping—even to sleep. Users call this "going on a run" or "tweaking." When they finally do stop using, they come down off the high even harder. Then they can become very angry, hostile, and depressed.

Going Through Withdrawal

When a person who abuses drugs suddenly stops taking them, his or her body goes through withdrawal. Withdrawal is when a person's body has adapted to functioning with drugs inside it. Without the drugs, the body goes into a sort of shock.

As with addiction, there are both physical and psychological effects involved in withdrawal. These include depression, paranoia, violence, anger, aggression, psychotic behavior, irritability, lack of energy, increased appetite, fear, and shaking. Withdrawal is so painful that some people will do almost anything to get more drugs; they may rob people, write bad checks, or shoplift. Fifty percent of violent crimes are committed when the offender is under the influence of drugs.

Symptoms of withdrawal are aches and pains, severe headache, cold sweats, and more. These effects are often extremely painful.

When someone chooses to stop using stimulants, it's important that he or she does it safely. With enough support and information, a person can handle the symptoms of withdrawal. Talking to parents, friends, a teacher, or a guidance counselor can help. There are also many organizations listed in the "For More Information" section of this book that are available to help.

The Process of Addiction

What if you're not sure whether you really are addicted to stimulants? You may have tried speed at a party. You may use drugs off and on, whenever you run into someone who is selling them. You think you have everything under control. But do you? The scary thing about addiction is that it usually happens without anyone realizing it. Like other addictions, stimulant addiction occurs in stages, as follows:

Stage 1: Experimentation
Stage 2: Regular use
Stage 3: Harmful involvement
Stage 4: Chemical dependence

The time it takes to go through these stages is different for each person. It can take only a month or two to become addicted to stimulants.

Why People Abuse Stimulants

You may turn to drugs to ease conflict and unhappiness. You may also be reacting to stressful situations in your life. Every user has a different reason for turning to drugs. But most people who use drugs have one thing in common—their drug use is only part of their problem. Looking at your emotions and the

DO YOU HAVE A DRUG PROBLEM?

Are you wondering whether you have a drug problem? Ask yourself these questions:

- Are you worried about your drug use?

- Is someone who cares about you worried about your drug use?

- Do you tell lies to cover it up?

- Do you feel like you can't get through the day without drugs?

- Have your friends stopped wanting to hang out with you?

- Are you missing a lot of school?

- Are you not doing as well in school as you used to?

- Have you stopped participating in activities (like sports) that you used to enjoy?

- Do you get extremely tired?

- Has your appetite changed a lot?

- Have you lost weight?

- Do you get irritated easily?

- Have you done things you normally wouldn't have done or things you wish you hadn't done?

world around you is an important part of dealing with a drug problem.

A person can feel lonely because of missing friends who have gone away. It's also not always a positive thing to be changing schools or work or other interests like sports or clubs. A person who is lonely may become sad or depressed. It's not easy to know what could be done to feel better and more interested in life. Some people who are lonely are vulnerable to any suggestion for a quick answer that might make them feel better right away. Some dealers make a point of offering drugs to lonely people who don't have friends to remind them to look for healthy choices instead.

There are many reasons why addiction can go hand in hand with family problems Some families find it hard to talk about feelings and worries. Teens may turn to drugs to escape unhappiness at home. In some families, drugs may be abused by a parent. Parents may even supply their teenagers with drugs or leave drugs where the teens can find them.

Drug abuse may be a family's way of coping with problems. Some families never talk about or deal with problems. Instead, they turn to drugs in order to forget. But drugs only make things worse.

You probably have felt down in the dumps or blue at different times in your life. It's natural to feel this way once in a while. You may have broken up with a boyfriend or girlfriend or lost a big game. Usually the hurt passes and life goes on. But what if

Since amphetamines and stimulants alter the chemistry of the brain, they can often cause lasting psychological damage, including depression.

the feeling just doesn't go away? You may not want to eat or even get out of bed. You may have trouble concentrating and feel hopeless most of the time.

Depression is a common psychological disorder that can be treated. The best way to get help is to approach a counselor at school or tell your parents. Sometimes it helps to talk to a therapist about your feelings. If you find you need additional help, there are several medications that a doctor or psychiatrist can prescribe for you, in combination with a nutritious diet and healthy activities.

You should never use amphetamines or other stimulants in order to treat depression yourself. They will only make your symptoms worse because every high is followed by a crash. If you and your doctor decide to treat your depression with medication, many different kinds of medication can help. Work with your doctor to find which one is best for you.

One of the best things you can do is talk about your feelings and what's going on in your life with someone who will listen. Find someone close to you whom you can trust.

5

OVERCOMING ADDICTION

D rug abuse is a very difficult problem to tackle. For many abusers, the hardest part is admitting that they need help. Most drug abusers think that drugs help them to be better people—they think they are more capable, more social, and more successful when they are high, so they cannot imagine being clean and sober. Drug abusers think that without their drugs, they will be unable to continue their daily lives. But that isn't true at all.

Addiction to amphetamines and stimulants is a serious problem that can rarely be tackled without help. It's important to speak to a professional about breaking the habit.

Some people think that they can kick their drug habit on their own. They may be embarrassed to get outside help, or they may feel as though it's no one's business but their own. But drug addiction has to be treated, physically and mentally. The body needs to detoxify, or get rid of the drug. Sometimes a stay in a hospital or clinic is needed in order to detoxify. This is customary. And it helps to have people around you who are struggling with the same kinds of problems as you are.

Getting off drugs can be painful, both physically and mentally. Having others around to help you will increase your chances of kicking the habit successfully. There are a number of drug treatment options available for those who are ready to get help.

You can talk to counselors about your problems. Counselors can help you start to think about why you're using drugs. A good counselor can help you identify real solutions to your problems. You can talk honestly with a counselor without having to worry about hurting his or her feelings or what he or she will think of you. Laws prevent counselors from discussing with other people the things that you tell them, so it's safe to talk about anything that's on your mind.

Self-help groups usually have three or four goals that members want to achieve, such as learning how to manage emotions and behavior in ways that are healthy. The groups focus on giving members the tools they need to deal with their problems and urges. Group sessions help members feel confident that they don't need a drug to get through hard times. Addicts learn they will have the personal power and support

Self-help groups are easy to find. You can use the traditional phone book or, more likely, the Internet to look up addresses and other information about them.

to face problems. Self-help groups can be found in the Yellow Pages, in the newspaper, or on the Internet.

Twelve-step programs, such as Narcotics Anonymous, have been very successful at helping people stay drug-free. They can help people develop the tools needed to stay sober. Members work through twelve specific steps toward recovery, beginning by admitting that they have a problem. Meetings are free and open to anyone struggling with addiction. Twelve-step programs can also be found in the newspaper, in the phone book, or on the Internet.

Choosing the Right Course

People need different kinds of support in order to break their addictions. Some people feel more support in self-help groups or twelve-step programs because they are meeting others who are in the same situation. Others need individual attention because they don't feel comfortable discussing their personal life in a group. Some teens may feel that an adult cannot under-stand what they're going through; instead, they might meet with a peer counselor.

Some people believe that just talking to friends will help them kick their drug addiction. But a friend may not have the resources or experience to provide you with the best advice. A professional can help you deal with the problems that are mak-ing you turn to drugs.

Expectations

Getting off drugs is more than just a single action—it's a pro-cess. While it involves stopping the physical use of the drug, it also requires getting to the root of why your drug problem began in the first place. Part of drug treatment is figuring out some of the reasons why you abused drugs and then learning

HAVING A LONG-RANGE VIEW

Having a long-range view means seeing the big picture. You have probably seen movies about other people's lives. If you could see a movie of how things were going to turn out for you, would it affect the way you live today? Of course it would. If you knew you were going to have an unsuccessful career because you used drugs when you were young, would you use them anyway? If you knew that you would become permanently paralyzed after a bad dose of drugs, would you continue to use them? If you knew that drugs would kill parts of your brain every time you used them, would you go on?

If you have a long-range view, you can see that using drugs hurts your chances of success in life. Counselors often refer to addicts as chronic underachievers. Addicts never get as far as they could have.

Being assertive means telling people what you want and what you do not want. It means saying no and meaning it. It means refusing to use drugs, or it means ending your use of drugs. Assertiveness can be difficult at first, but it gets easier with practice. When you first use assertiveness, drug dealers (who can be your peers or friends, too) will try to make you give in. If you continue to say no, they will leave you alone.

Parents and other adults can help you find ways to deal with peer pressure. Pastors, rabbis, teachers, and grandparents

Even if you are able to get off drugs, the temptations will always be around. The most powerful weapon you have is the ability to walk away.

have had years of experience dealing with things like peer pressure. (Yes, even they had problems with peer pressure.) You can ask a younger adult whom you respect for advice, or ask him or her to come with you when you consult someone else. You may be surprised how well their advice works.

Amphetamines and other stimulants are very dangerous substances. When you're feeling depressed or overwhelmed, the kind of effects they promise can seem appealing, but the long-term effects can be devastating. You have alternatives.

to deal with these reasons constructively. This takes time. It's important to be realistic about just how much time it will take to figure out those problems. Setting unreasonable expectations for yourself can make you depressed when you find that you're unable to meet them, and that can bring you back to the kind of situation that led to your drug use in the first place. Give yourself enough time to really recover from your addiction so that you can move forward with confidence.

It can be tough to return to a social life after rehabilitation. Others may seem to be using drugs without any problems. Don't be fooled. Remember that a combination of determination and support from family, friends, and other sources can help you stick to your recovery. The recovery process is a long one. But it helps to remember that recovery is helping you regain control of your life.

Overcoming Pressure

Peer pressure could be one reason why you start using drugs. Other teens may try to convince you to use drugs because everyone else is. If you refuse, they may try to make you feel like an outcast. As a teen, you face peer pressure from many different sources.

You want the other kids to respect you. But where does respect come from? It starts with self-respect. Would you respect someone who didn't respect himself or herself? Do

Peer pressure is yet another temptation that former drug users must deal with. Part of breaking the cycle of addiction is learning how to avoid these pressures.

you respect people who use drugs? Would others respect you if you used drugs? How would you feel about yourself if you became addicted?

Let's face it: no one likes to be criticized. Being made fun of can be painful. But what do teens think of their peers who use and abuse drugs? Do they make friends with the speed freaks or the stoners? Or do they criticize them? Statistics from an ongoing series of surveys by the National Institutes of Health show that more than 80 percent of twelfth-grade students disapprove of amphetamine abuse.

Some people get addicted to drugs because dealers (also called pushers) pressure them. Dealers are very good at that. They can make you feel stupid or weak if you don't try drugs.

Dealers have many ways to get teens hooked on drugs. It is their job. They may threaten to hurt you or someone you care about. They may give you free samples. They will do whatever they can in order to get you hooked. Once you're addicted, they know you'll buy again and again. Your addiction means more money in their pockets.

Peer pressure can be difficult to beat. There are ways to beat it, though, including these suggestions. It is important to have a sense of who you are. Psychologists call this concept having a sense of identity. It means knowing what you want out of life.

Do you want to be an airline pilot? An army officer? A senator? An athlete or a scientist? Drugs could ruin your chances to be any of those things. If you know who you are and what you want, it will be hard for anyone to push you into taking drugs.

GLOSSARY

addiction A state or condition of being unable to stop using a drug.

amphetamines Powerful synthetic stimulants; a number of drugs popularly known as speed.

binge A period of excessive use. A speed binge may last from three to fifteen days and is followed by a period of exhaustion known as a crash.

coma A state of unconsciousness as a result of a disease, an accident, or a poison.

convulsion A involuntary and violent spasm of the muscles.

crash The depression that hits stimulant abusers when coming down from a high.

crystal meth The street name for a combination of methedrine and amphetamine; also called methamphetamine.

detoxify The process of removing drugs from the body.

dosage The amount of a drug used at one time.

drug abuse The use of a drug in a manner or for a purpose other than that for which it is prescribed.

euphoria An exaggerated feeling of well-being that has no basis in reality.

hallucination Something seen or felt that does not exist outside the mind.

ice A smokeable form of methamphetamine.

neurotransmitter A chemical that transmits signals between nerve cells.

run A period of several days of drug use without sleep.

rush The sudden feeling of euphoria associated with smoking or injecting a drug.

seizure A spasm of the body.

speed Stimulants such as amphetamine or methamphetamine; slang for drugs that excite the mind and body; also called uppers.

speedball A combination of speed and heroin.

speed freak A habitual speed user.

tolerance The body's ability to get used to, or become less responsive to, a drug, requiring larger doses to get the same effect.

tweaking Another term for going on a run; using stimulants over and over without stopping.

uppers Slang for drugs that excite the mind and body; also called speed.

withdrawal The physical effects experienced when giving up drugs.

FOR MORE INFORMATION

American Council for Drug Education (ACDE)
164 West 74th Street
New York, NY 10023
(800) DRUG-HELP (378-4435)
Web site: http://www.acde.org
The ACDE's Web site is still under construction. It
   will have useful information for young people,
   parents, teachers, and employers on programs
   to prevent substance abuse.

Narcotics Anonymous (NA)
P.O. Box 9999
Van Nuys, CA 91409
(818) 773-9999
Web site: http://www.na.org
This organization provides basic information
   about its twelve-step program, which is a non-
   profit self-help program for people who have
   problems with substance abuse.

National Center on Addiction & Substance Abuse
   (CASA)
Columbia University
633 Third Avenue, 19th Floor
New York, NY 10017–6706
(212) 841-5200

Web site: http://www.casacolumbia.org

CASA's Web site provides many links to articles and research
   reports by CASA members. It's a good resource for statistics and recent articles on abuse of stimulants and other
   substances.

National Clearinghouse for Alcohol and Drug Information
P.O. Box 2345
Rockville, MD 20847–2345
(800) 729-6686
Web site: http://ncadi.samhsa.gov

This agency is a good resource for government and private statistics on substance abuse.

National Council on Alcoholism and Drug Dependence
20 Exchange Place, Suite 2902
New York, NY 10005
(800) 622-2255
Web site: http://www.ncadd.org

This organization fights the stigma and the disease of alcoholism and other drug addictions. There are many links to local
   resources, useful Web sites, government programs, and
   treatment centers listed on its Web site.

National Institute on Drug Abuse (NIDA)
6001 Executive Boulevard, Room 5213
Bethesda, MD 20892–9651

(301) 443-1124

Web site: http://www.nida.nih.gov

NIDA is part of the National Institutes of Health of the U.S.
Department of Health and Human Services. Each of its
divisions and offices participates in programs of drug abuse
research. There is considerable useful material on the Web
site concerning amphetamine abuse and its treatment.

Toronto Area of Narcotics Anonymous

P.O. Box # 5700, Depot A

Toronto, ON M5W 1N8

Canada

(416) 236-8956

Web site: http://www.torontona.org/index.htm

Toronto Area of Narcotics Anonymous provides Toronto resi-
dents with resources to seek help for drug addiction.

Web Sites

Due to the changing nature of Internet links, Rosen Publishing
has developed an online list of Web sites related to the subject
of this book. This site is updated regularly. Please use this link to
access the list:

http://www.rosenlinks.com/dac/amph

FOR FURTHER READING

Bellenir, Karen. *Drug Information for Teens: Health Tips About the Physical and Mental Effects of Substance Abuse* (Teen Health). Detroit, MI: Omnigraphics, 2006.

Brady, Betty. *Meth Survivor: Jennifer's Story and How One Community Fought Back.* Bloomington, IN: Authorhouse, 2006.

Farren, Mick. *Speed-Speed-Speedfreak: A Fast History of Amphetamine.* Port Townsend, WA: Feral House, 2010.

Grilly, David M. *Drugs and Human Behavior.* Boston, MA: Allyn & Bacon, 2006.

Iversen, Leslie. *Speed, Ecstasy, Ritalin: The Science of Amphetamines.* New York, NY: Oxford University Press, 2008.

Johnson, Dirk. *Meth: America's Home-Cooked Menace.* Center City, MN: Hazelden Publishing, 2005.

Klosterman, Lorrie. *The Facts About Over-the-Counter Drugs.* New York, NY: Marshall Cavendish/Benchmark Press, 2007.

Kuhn, Cynthia, et al. *Buzzed: The Straight Facts About the Most Used and Abused Drugs from Alcohol to Ecstasy.* New York, NY: W. W. Norton & Company, 2008.

Lynn, Tracy. *Rx.* New York, NY: Simon & Schuster, 2005.

McCormick, Patricia. *My Brother's Keeper*. New York, NY: Hyperion Books for Children, 2005.

Menhard, Francha. *The Facts About Ritalin*. New York, NY: Benchmark Books, 2006.

Munoz, Mercedes. *What Causes Addiction?* Farmington Hills, MI: Greenhaven Press, 2005.

Owen, Frank. *No Speed Limit: Meth Across America*. New York, NY: St. Martin's Press, 2006.

Rasmussen, Nicolas. *On Speed: The Many Lives of Amphetamine*. New York, NY: NYU Press, 2009.

Salant, James. *Leaving Dirty Jersey: A Crystal Meth Memoir*. New York, NY: Simon Spotlight Entertainment, 2007.

Walker, Ida. *Recreational Ritalin: The Not-So-Smart Drug*. Broomall, PA: Mason Crest Publishers, 2007.

Watkins, Christine, ed. *Prescription Drugs*. San Diego, CA: Greenhaven Press, 2006

INDEX

About the Author

Nicolette P. Conti is a writer living in New Jersey.

Paula Johanson is the author of several wellness titles, including *Breast Cancer Prevention* and *Recipe for Disaster: Processed Food*.

Photo Credits

Cover, pp. 1, 7, 18, 27, 38, 46, 56, 58, 61, 63 © www.istockphoto.com/FotografiaBasica; p. 4–5 Cordelia Molloy/Photo Researchers; p. 10 © Monica Almeida/The New York Times/Redux Pictures; pp. 13, 33 istockphoto/Thinkstock; p. 15 William F. Campbell/ Time & Life Images/Time & Life Pictures/Getty Images; p. 16 NY Daily News Archive/NY Daily News via Getty Images; p. 20 Dennis R. Cain-CRA/Custom Medical Stock Photo; pp. 25, 28, 40, 44, 49, 54 Shutterstock; p. 30 Craig Zuckerman/Visuals Unlimited/Getty Images; p. 47 © www.istockphoto.com/Chris Schmidt; p. 52 © Spencer Grant/Photo Edit.

Editor: Nick Croce; Photo Researcher: Marty Levick